I0161414

In Defense of
The King James Bible

"For thou art my lamp, O LORD" (2 Sam. 22:29).
"God is light,
and <u>in him is no darkness at all</u>" (1 John 1:5).
"Teach me <u>thy way</u>, O LORD; I will walk <u>in thy truth</u>:
unite my heart to fear thy name.
I will praise thee, O Lord my God, with all my heart:
and I will glorify thy name for evermore"
(Ps. 86:11–12).
"Then Simon Peter answered him, Lord,
to whom shall we go?
<u>thou hast the words of eternal life</u>"
(John 6:68)

Rick Streight

TEACH Services, Inc.
P U B L I S H I N G
www.TEACHServices.com ● (800) 367-1844

Copyright © 2012, 2022 Rick Streight and TEACH Services, Inc.

ISBN-13: 978-1-57258-944-5 (Paperback)

ISBN-13: 978-1-57258-926-1 (Hardback)

ISBN-13: 978-1-57258-843-1 (ePub)

Library of Congress Control Number: 2012945646

All scripture quotations, unless otherwise indicated, are taken from the King James Version Bible.

Scripture quotations marked GNB are taken from the Good News Bible © 1994 published by the Bible Societies/HarperCollins Publishers Ltd UK, Good News Bible © American Bible Society 1966, 1971, 1976, 1992. Used with permission.

J. B. Phillips, "The New Testament in Modern English," 1962 edition, published by HarperCollins.

Scripture quotations marked (NIV) are taken from the Holy Bible, New International Version®, NIV®. Copyright © 1973, 1978, 1984 by Biblica, Inc.™ Used by permission of Zondervan. All rights reserved worldwide.

Revised Standard Version of the Bible, copyright 1952 [2nd edition, 1971] by the Division of Christian Education of the National Council of the Churches of Christ in the United States of America. Used by permission. All rights reserved

Scripture quotations marked "TLB" or "The Living Bible" are taken from The Living Bible / Kenneth N. Taylor. electronic ed. Wheaton Tyndale House, 1997, c1971 by Tyndale House Publishers, Inc. Used by permission. All rights reserved.

All bold or underlining in Bible texts are supplied by the author.

TEACH Services, Inc.

P U B L I S H I N G

www.TEACHServices.com • (800) 367-1844

Dedication

I dedicate this book to God's brethren and sisters in the faith of Jesus, like myself, who desire a better understanding of what it means to be a Christian, fighting the good fight of faith (see 2 Tim. 4:7–8) and hastening Jesus' second coming. After his conversion, Peter wrote, "Looking for and hasting unto the coming of the day of God ... Nevertheless we, according to his promise, look for new heavens and a new earth, wherein dwelleth righteousness. Wherefore, beloved, seeing that ye look for such things, be diligent that ye may be found of him [Jesus] in peace, without spot, and blameless" (2 Peter 3:12–14).

This book is also dedicated to the work of those who produced the first King James Bible. The first Bible to have the text divided into verses was the Geneva Bible, known as the Reformation Bible, AD 1560–1644. It was at this time that Protestant King James of Scotland and England, during the reformation, wanted to restore Christian unity and truth to his kingdom. Thus, he decided to produce an English translation of the Bible, and for more than two and a half centuries, no other translation was made in England. The beloved King James Bible became the "authorized version" of the English-speaking people. It took fifty scholars seven years and was completed in AD 1611.

In the United States, when swearing in a president, all the way back to George Washington, the president-elect puts his hand on the King James Bible to make a promise (oath) to our country and God. When going to court to stand before the judge, witnesses put their hand on the Bible and promise to tell the "truth, the whole truth, and nothing but the truth, so help me God" before they give their testimony. Although we can't always trust one another, we should be able to trust the Word of God—the Bible.

Table of Contents

Introduction 7

Acknowledgements 15

CHAPTER 1
Principles Need to Be Applied to Come
to a Correct Understanding of Bible Truth............ 17

CHAPTER 2
Jesus Christ: The Word of God............................ 21

CHAPTER 3
Feeding and Protecting the Flock of God 27

CHAPTER 4
Warnings Against Altering the Bible.................... 31

CHAPTER 5
God's Pure, Preserved, and Unadulterated Word 37

CHAPTER 6
God is Not the Author of Confusion..................... 47

CHAPTER 7
Can the King James Version Bible
Be Understood? 49

CHAPTER 8
Beware of Satan's Deceptions 53

Chapter 9
The Facts: A Comparison of Bible Translations 57

CHAPTER 10
Loyalty to God 92

Introduction

Dear precious brethren and sisters in the faith,

Revival and reformation are needed in our churches today, and I believe in my heart this will only come about as we read God's truths in the preserved Word of God.

As I write this introductory letter, I am reminded of just how much God loves us and wants to save us. The Bible confirms how much God cares for us: "Since thou wast precious in my sight, thou hast been honourable, and I have loved thee" (Isa. 43:4); "Yea, I have loved thee with an everlasting love" (Jer. 31:3); "We love him, because he first loved us" (1 John 4:19).

From my study of reading the Bible for more than thirty years, I am convinced that God is not looking for ways to keep us out of heaven— that's the devil's job. "The thief cometh not, but for to steal, and to kill, and to destroy: I am come that they might have life, and that they might have it more abundantly. I am the good shepherd" (John 10:10–11).

God wants us to spend eternity with Him; He loves us! The beloved disciple John says it like this: "For God sent not his Son [Jesus] into the world to condemn the world; but that the world through him might be saved" (John 3:17).

In reference to the church of God, Paul wrote, "These things write I unto thee, hoping to come unto thee shortly: But if I tarry long, that thou mayest know how thou oughtest to behave thyself in the house of God, which is the church of the living God, the pillar and ground of the truth" (1 Tim. 3:14–15). Truth is very important! God knows it, and Satan knows it, too. When truth is revealed, it exposes him as a liar and a deceiver, and he doesn't like that!

We all have Bibles we love to read that have taught us about salvation and have been a blessing to us, some translations more than others, as you will see in this study. Have you ever wondered why there are so many Christian churches in the world that believe so differently? Be careful! Paul knew he was going to die; he had to pass the torch of truth on to Timothy. When Timothy died, he passed the torch of truth to you and me. Paul wrote, "For the time will come when they will not endure sound doctrine; but after their own lusts shall they heap to themselves teachers, having itching ears; and they shall turn away their ears from the truth, and shall be turned unto fables. But watch thou in all things, endure afflictions, do the work of an evangelist, make full proof of thy ministry" (2 Tim. 4:3–5). Paul told Timothy to not compromise or water down the truth. Timothy is telling us the same thing!

This book is not an attack on godly Christians. We are all traveling the path of sanctification, learning God's will for our lives. This book is about unmasking Satan's attempt to minimize God's power in the Word of God and making us aware that not all Bibles are faithful to "the truth [as it] is in Jesus" (Eph. 4:21).

If we want to be used by God, we must study the Bible and be prepared to share what we learn with others: "Thy word is truth" (John 17:17), not a mixture of truth and error. King David understood the importance of following God's commands and growing in knowledge: "The fear of the LORD is the beginning of wisdom: a good understanding have all they that do his commandments: his praise endureth for ever" (Ps. 111:10).

Jesus Christ was the love of God manifested to mankind. He showed us the Father's will and paid the penalty of our sins in His own body: "In this was manifested the love of God toward us, because that God sent his only begotten Son into the world, that we might live through him. Herein is love, not that we loved God, but that he loved us, and sent his Son to be the propitiation [remedy] for our sins" (1 John 4:9–10).

It is humbling to think that Christ bore our sins for us. In 1 Peter 2:24–25, we read the following: "Who his own self bare our sins in his own body on the tree, that we, being dead to sins, should live unto righteousness: by whose stripes ye are healed. For ye were [past tense] as sheep going astray; but are now [present tense] returned unto the Shepherd and Bishop of our souls." These verses of Scripture became personal to me when I contemplated Calvary and how much Jesus suffered because of your sins and mine. David says it like this: "Create in me a clean heart, O God; and renew a right spirit within me" (Ps. 51:10). Read also Isaiah 53. When you do, you will say goodbye to the world and will say hello to Jesus. As I have grown in my relationship with

Christ, my desire has increased to want to read the Bible translation that most correctly represents God's will for my life. When I think of Jesus, it is not the fear of punishment or the reward of everlasting life that makes me want to follow Him. I want to be more and more like Him because I have fallen in love with Him, and I desire a lasting relationship with Him. God's Word is so true: "O taste and see that the LORD is good: blessed is the man that trusteth in him" (Ps. 34:8); "And ye shall seek me, and find me, when ye shall search for me with all your heart" (Jer. 29:13).

David is an example to all of us. In God's Word, he defines what it means to love God: "Restore unto me the joy of thy salvation; and uphold me with thy free spirit. Then will I teach transgressors thy ways; and sinners shall be converted unto thee" (Ps. 51:12–13).

As we continue the upward climb of sanctification, we develop a strong loyalty and bond to our heavenly Father. But because Satan hates the Word of God, we must be on guard "Lest Satan should get an advantage of us: for we are not ignorant of his devices" (2 Cor. 2:11). In this passage Paul is reminding us to believe in the Word of God. "For therein is the righteousness of God revealed from faith to faith: as it is written, The just shall live by faith" (Rom. 1:17). In spite of all of Satan's efforts, God has promised us that He will preserve the Word of God: "The words of the LORD are pure words: as silver tried in a furnace of earth, purified seven times. Thou shalt keep them, O LORD, thou shalt preserve them from this generation for ever" (Ps. 12:6–7). God does not lie. I believe it because He said so (see Titus 1:1–2; Heb. 6:18).

A number of years ago, I read a book on the differences in Bible translations, and I was shocked when I investigated the facts. I bought eight different popular translations of the New Testament and compared the Bibles with the King James Version. In these modern versions, I discovered red flags from different wordings that I believe do not correctly represent the truth that our Lord and Savior inspired the Bible writers to pen.

It's interesting to note that for more than 300 years, the King James Version was the Reformation Bible used by Protestants to proclaim the truths of the Bible. Time has caused many to forget the price people have paid to uphold the truth of God's Word. Revival and reformation came about as a result of godly men such as John Wycliffe, William Tyndale, and Martin Luther standing up for truth and making the Bible available in the language of the common people. Many were tortured and put to death because of their religious beliefs. They were called heretics, but many became martyrs for their faith. The Bible and its truths were very important to them—may the Bible and its truth be important to us, too. God's Word says, "Through thy precepts I get understanding: therefore I hate every false way" (Ps. 119:104). We enjoy religious liberty today because of those faithful men who thought truth was important enough to stand up for and even die for.

The King James Bible lifts up and exalts our Lord and Savior Jesus Christ. This is the standard of God's faithful and genuine Bible. "Search the scriptures; for in them ye think ye have eternal life: and they are they which testify of me" (John 5:39). The preserved and faithful Bible that we can trust for sound doctrine will always exalt Jesus and His Deity and His power to forgive us and give us victory over sin, uphold His virgin birth, teach the importance of His blood atonement, and not water down our blessed hope of Jesus' second coming (see Ps. 73:24)!

As Christianity has increased in popularity, more and more modern translations of the Bible have been written with the thought that they are easier to understand. I like that! But Satan is not stupid—he is a deceiver, a liar. The majority of these Bible translations present a lot of truth, but what most people don't know is that some false teachings or doctrines have also been introduced by changing the words and phrases, thus allowing private interpretation to influence what Christians believe. Therefore, truth has been changed, and God's people are in grave danger unless men and women, like you and me, sound the trumpet and warn others about Satan's attempts to confuse and deceive. It is getting harder to find a King James Version Bible in Christian bookstores, and someone needs to promote this faithful and true Bible translation.

This book may not be popular, but I cannot be silent. Please do not take offense to what I have written, for I love God, His church, and my fellow brothers and sisters in Christ. I love the Word of God, the blueprint to salvation through Christ Jesus: "And that from a child thou hast known the holy scriptures, which are able to make thee wise unto salvation through faith which is in Christ Jesus" (2 Tim. 3:15). I encourage all serious and faithful Christians to take the time to investigate the facts of what you will read in the coming pages. I am not a King James Version Bible only advocate, but I am an advocate of the truth. So which Bible is faithful to the truth as was written by the authors of the Bible?

I encourage you to put aside all preconceived ideas and suspend final judgment until all of the evidence is in. Please do not pass judgment upon this study until you have prayerfully read all of it! King Solomon, the wisest man who ever lived, wrote, "He that answereth a matter before he heareth it, it is folly and shame unto him" (Prov. 18:13).

We owe the devil no loyalty at all. He is the archenemy of God. He knows that worldly people will be lost and will miss out on eternal life. But he is greedy; he also wants Christians to be lost too! If possible, he will pervert Scripture. And the facts prove that he has been very successful. May we thank God for exposing Satan's methods to hinder our ability to be sanctified to God's glory and His vindication. In Christian love for the brethren who "keep the commandments of God, and the faith of Jesus" (Rev. 14:12), may you read and understand the points that are presented in this book.

In God's Service,

Rick Martin Streight

Acknowledgements

There have been many influences that led me to write this book. While reading God's Word with a heartfelt desire to know Jesus better, I learned things in the King James Bible that were so precious to me that I wrote them down. Then the Holy Spirit convicted me to share what I had learned with others. Truth will never contradict itself because Jesus is truth (see John 14:6), and doctrine is important (see 2 Tim. 4:1–8).

My relationship with God started fifty-plus years ago at 332 West Potomac Street in Brunswick, Maryland. I thank God for the early growing-up years with my grandma, Wilma Dolly Streight. She made sure we went to church every week. The memories of her love, unselfishness, and sacrificial willingness to take care of her family and grandchildren, which included my brother, Mike, my sister, Barbara, and myself, are things I passed on to my family. My grandma was my first impression of what God is like before I ever opened up a Bible. I will never forget those wonderful memories!

I thank my dear wife, Theresa, for being faithful and patient with me, giving me good advice, helping me spell words correctly, and spending long hours on the computer putting the rough copy together for me to submit to TEACH Services for publication.

And finally, I want to acknowledge the faithfulness of the "cloud of witnesses" (see Heb. 11; 12:1) and the martyrs of the Protestant Reformation who chose to die rather than compromise truth or sin against God. They taught me to have a strong spiritual backbone, even if the truth is not popular.

Chapter 1

Principles Need to Be Applied to Come to a Correct Understanding of Bible Truth

"Study to shew thyself approved unto God, a workman that needeth not to be ashamed, rightly dividing the word of truth" (2 Tim. 2:15).

"For I will give you a mouth and wisdom, which all your adversaries shall not be able to gainsay nor resist" (Luke 21:15).

"These were more noble than those in Thessalonica, in that they received the word with all readiness of mind, and searched the scriptures daily, whether those things were so" (Acts 17:11).

"But He [Jesus] answered and said, It is written, Man shall not live by bread alone, but by every word that proceedeth out of the mouth of God." (Matt. 4:4).

About believers in Christ: "They are not of the world, even as I am not of the world. Sanctify them through thy truth: thy word is truth" (John 17:16–17).

Because so many churches do not agree on doctrine (truth), forty-plus years ago I started a deep study of the King James Bible, trusting the Holy Spirit as my teacher. As we prepare for doing God's will and spending eternity with God, we must seek God's counsel to guard against private interpretation.

Now, for confidence and safety, here are the principles we can follow that will "unite us in truth and glorify the Father" (see John 17:1–11, 20–21).

Fact: believing something, especially when it is popular does not mean it is the truth. Paul told us to "Prove all things; hold fast that which is good" (1 Thess. 5:21). You might ask, Lord, how do we study Your Word with confidence and assurance? Our heavenly Father (God) answers us in Isaiah 28:9–10. He asked: "Whom shall he teach knowledge? and whom shall he make to understand doctrine?" And the answer is, "them that are weaned from the milk, and drawn from the breasts." Ask God for wisdom to mature your Christian experience. "For precept must be upon precept, precept upon precept; line upon line, line upon line; here a little, and there a little."

There is danger when we go to church every week and don't actually read God's Word on a prayerful, daily basis. Isolated scripture is never God's appointed way for us to come to a correct understanding of truth. We can easily come to a wrong conclusion. With the help of an exhaustive concordance, Bible dictionary, and prayer, we are to hear all truth available, open-minded, "reasoning together" (see Isa. 1:18) is the Bible way. No debating—I'm right, you're wrong, etc. God wants us to seek Christian unity in truth (see John 17:17). To "God's glory" (see John 17:22).

King Solomon, the wisest king who ever lived (he asked God for wisdom) said this: "He that answereth a matter before he heareth it, it is folly and shame unto him" (Prov. 18:13). Paul gave us added insight: "Now we have received, not the spirit of the world, but the spirit which is of God; that we might know the things that are freely given to us of God. Which things also we speak, not in the words which man's wisdom teacheth, but which the Holy Ghost teacheth; comparing spiritual things with spiritual" (1 Cor. 2:12–13).

The early Christians were commended in this practice: "These were more noble than those in Thessalonica, in that they received the word with all readiness of mind, and searched the scriptures daily, whether those things were so" (Acts 17:11). In Matthew 4:1 it says this: "Then was Jesus led up of the Spirit into the wilderness to be tempted of the devil." Amazingly, the devil quoted Scripture but out of context. Jesus, "our example" (see 1 Peter 2:21), quoted more Scripture to prove the devil wrong and to teach what was correct.

CHAPTER 2

Jesus Christ: The Word of God

As we begin this study, I want to focus on the integrity of Jesus as the Word of God. Jesus, the Son of God, came to reveal His Father's character on this earth. "Jesus saith unto him, I am the way, the truth, and the life: no man cometh unto the Father, but by me" (John 14:6).

Jesus Is the Word of God to Christians

Jesus validated the Scriptures and used them to verify who He was: "Search the scriptures; for in them ye think ye have eternal life: and they are they which testify of me" (John 5:39).

Although the religious leaders as a rule did not accept Jesus as the Messiah, many other Jews who had studied the Scriptures believed and embraced His teachings. In the first chapter of the gospel of John, further validation is presented as to Jesus' position as the Word of God: "In the beginning was the Word, and the Word was with God, and the Word was God. And the Word was made flesh, and dwelt among us, (and we beheld his glory, the glory as of the only begotten of the Father,) full of grace and truth" (John 1:1, 14).

While on earth, Jesus instilled in His disciples the importance of having a personal relationship with the Son of God. Jesus said, "I am the bread of life.... He that eateth my flesh, and drinketh my blood, dwelleth in me, and I in him.... It is the spirit that quickeneth; the flesh profiteth nothing: the words that I speak unto you, they are spirit, and they are life.... Then Simon Peter answered him, Lord, to whom shall we go? thou hast the words of eternal life" (John 6:48–68).

Jesus, the Word of God, Is Faithful and True

After Jesus' resurrection, He returned to His Father in heaven, but He left His Word, the Bible, with His people to strengthen and guide us along our spiritual journey. Among many things, the Bible regenerates us, encourages us, convicts us of sin, and reproves us. Yes, the Word of God has been magnified above the name of Jesus. This is why the Psalmist David wrote, "For thou hast magnified thy word above all thy name" (Ps. 138:2).

In Revelation 19:11–13 in the King James Bible, John speaks to the authority of the Word of God and validates its truth: "And I saw heaven opened, and behold a white horse; and he that sat upon him was called Faithful and True, and in righteousness he doth judge and make war. His eyes were as a flame of fire, and on his head were many crowns; and he had a name written, that no man knew, but he himself. And he was clothed with a vesture dipped in blood: and his name is called The Word of God.".

The Purpose of Reading the Bible

The purpose of the Bible is to give us hope and an understanding of our Creator and Savior. The Bible points us to God and the gift of His Son. "Jesus saith unto him, Thomas, because thou hast seen me, thou hast believed: blessed are they that have not seen, and yet have believed. And many other signs truly did Jesus in the presence of his disciples, which are not written in this book: But these are written, that ye might believe that Jesus is the Christ, the Son of God; and that believing ye might have life through his name" (John 20:29–31).

Protecting the Flock from Satan's Errors, Deceptions, and Power

Jesus seeks to protect His followers from Satan through the truths presented in the Bible. With the Word of God as our guide, we can have victory over the devil's attacks. However, in order to be victorious, we must prayerfully and obediently study the Bible and embrace its teachings.

The apostle Paul gives us very important counsel in this regard: "And that from a child thou hast known the holy scriptures, which are able to make thee wise unto salvation through faith which is in Christ Jesus. All scripture is given by inspiration of God, and is profitable for doctrine, for reproof, for correction, for instruction in righteousness: that the man of God may be perfect [mature], thoroughly furnished unto all good works" (2 Tim. 3:15–17). Because the inspired writings of the Bible are critical to our understanding of God and what He asks of us, it is so important that we read a translation of the Bible we can trust, one that correctly reflects Jesus as "the truth" (see John 14:6). As we carefully study the Word, we will be sanctified by the truth (see John 17:17).

David counsels us: "Wherewithal shall a young man cleanse his way? by taking heed thereto according to thy word.... Thy word have I hid in mine heart [not just head knowledge], that I might not sin against thee" (Ps. 119:9, 11).

Doers Verses Hearers

Moses counseled the children of Israel to follow the instructions the Lord had provided them. "Now therefore hearken, O Israel [the church], unto the statutes and unto the judgments, which I teach you, <u>for to do</u> <u>them</u>, that ye may live, and go in and possess the land which the LORD God of your fathers giveth you. <u>Ye shall not add unto the word which I command you, neither shall ye diminish ought from it</u>, that ye may keep the commandments of the LORD your God which I command you" (Deut. 4:1–2, emphasis supplied).

Similarly, James instructed believers in the early church to wholeheartedly follow the Word of God: "But be ye doers of the word, and not hearers only, deceiving your own selves" (James 1:22).

The beloved John celebrated the fact that Christ's followers were worshiping in spirit and in truth! He wrote, "I rejoiced greatly that I found of thy children <u>walking in truth</u>, as we have received a commandment from the Father" (2 John 4).

It may seem hard to imagine, but there are Bible translations that are leading people away from the truth! Examples of the discrepancies between various

Bible translations are revealed in chapter 9. You be the judge. These discrepancies can affect our victory over sin, our faith, and even our salvation. Satan wants us to distrust God's Word—we need not fall into his trap.

Fortunately, despite Satan's attempt to discredit the Bible, God has faithfully preserved His Word, and He is preparing a people to spend eternity with Him. I urge you to study this issue for yourself.

CHAPTER 3

Feeding and Protecting the Flock of God

Not only did God provide us with His Word and the Holy Spirit after Jesus ascended to heaven but He also gave us church leaders to instruct and protect us as we grow. "Be thou diligent to know the state of thy flocks, and look well to thy herds" (Prov. 27:23). Guiding the church and its members is a serious job that God has bestowed upon certain individuals.

The book of Acts contains instruction and guidance for **faithful church leaders**:

> Take heed therefore unto yourselves, and to all the flock, over the which the Holy Ghost hath made you overseers, to feed the church of God, which he hath purchased with his own blood. For I know this, that after my departing shall grievous wolves enter in among you, not sparing the flock. Also of your own selves shall men arise, speaking perverse things, to draw away disciples after them. Therefore watch, and remember, that by the space of three years I ceased not to warn every one night and day

with tears. And now, brethren, I commend you to God, and to the word of his grace, which is able to build you up, and to give you an inheritance among all them which are sanctified.... I have shewed you all things, how that so labouring ye ought to support the weak, and to remember the words of the Lord Jesus, how he said, It is more blessed to give than to receive. (Acts 20:28–35)

Scripture clearly states that the church leaders (overseers) and those who are spiritually mature must feed and protect the weaker brethren, who we sometimes refer to as "babes in Christ" (1 Cor. 3:1, 2). Peter reminds us that we are not to be lords over other members, we are to be good examples, models of God's character and faithful to His Word: "Neither as being lords over God's heritage, but being examples to the flock" (1 Peter 5:3).

As leaders and members seek to encourage and guide those around them, they must follow Jesus' example of encouragement. Jesus knew that His life was a living testament of God: "Behold, a virgin shall be with child, and shall bring forth a son, and they shall call his name Emmanuel, which being interpreted is, God with us" (Matt. 1:23). Jesus showed us God's character in all that He did: "And for their sakes I sanctify myself, that they also might be sanctified through the truth" (John 17:19).

Like Jesus correctly represented His Father's character, we who call ourselves Christians are to correctly represent Jesus' character. But Satan hates us, so we must keep our spiritual armor on and pray that we are mature leaders who are faithful to God's calling to feed and protect the flock and warn of danger.

Because of the important role church leaders play in guiding their flock, I urge all leaders to preach and teach from the King James Version Bible to minimize confusion and maximize the impact of the truths found in the Word of God.

Leaders and pastors have a big responsibility to be faithful to the truth and to point those who look up to "the way, the truth, and the life" (John 14:6). Salvation is at stake! May we humbly accept the reality of this clear truth in Scripture: "For the time has come that judgment must begin at the house of God: and if it first begin at us, what shall the end be of them that obey not the gospel of God? And if the righteous scarcely be saved, where shall the ungodly and the sinner appear? Wherefore let them that suffer according to the will of God commit the keeping of their souls to him [Jesus] in well doing, as unto a faithful Creator" (1 Peter 4:17–19).

CHAPTER 4

Warnings Against Altering the Bible

The Bible is so important to God's people that warnings have been given to anyone who would attempt to pervert Scripture by adding to or taking away from the truth. "Every word of God is pure: he is a shield unto them that put their trust in him. Add thou not unto his words, lest he reprove thee, and thou be found a liar" (Prov. 30:5–6).

In Deuteronomy 12:32 and Revelation 22:18–20, respectively, God commands us to guard His Word: "What thing soever I command you, observe to do it: thou shall not add thereto, nor diminish from it"; "For I testify unto every man that heareth the words of the prophecy of this book, If any man shall add unto these things, God shall add unto him the plagues that are written in this book: And if any man shall take away from the words of book of this prophecy, God shall take away his part out of the book of life, and out of the holy city, and from the things that are written in this book. He which testifieth these things sayeth, Surely I come quickly. Amen. Even so, come, Lord Jesus."

There are sincere Christians who like to point out that the word Easter in Acts 12:4 of the King James Bible is a mistranslation (error), saying that it should be replaced with the word Passover (Greek: *pascha*). But if you read closely, it says "after Easter." For this reason it should not be translated Passover <u>because the Passover was over</u>. The Passover always occurred on the fourteenth day of the month, while the days of the unleavened bread ran from the fifteenth through the twenty-first (Num. 28:16–18; Exod. 12:13–18).

King David also wrote about God's Word and the importance of its principles: "Through thy precepts I get understanding: therefore <u>I hate every false way</u>" (Ps. 119:104).

It has also been said that the King James Bible has added some words in italics. That statement is true, but these italicized words do not promote false doctrine or take away from the truth. Faithfulness to Jesus is upheld! Many Bibles add words you are not aware of that sometimes change the meaning of the Scripture. In contrast, when translating from one language to another, the King James Bible translators, honest and dedicated men of God, let us know which words they added in order to clarify the full meaning of the text by italicizing the words. No one has ever proven that the italicized words are not the Word of God. The original manuscripts are not available for comparison. Actually, they are words of God, compare the New Testament writers quoting the King James Bible in the Old Testament (Deut. 8:3; Matt. 4:4; Deut. 25:4; 1 Cor. 9:9; 1 Tim. 5:18; Isa. 28:16; 1 Peter 2:6). The italics were in the original manuscripts!

God predicted that there would be those who would counterfeit or attempt to pervert His pure and holy Word. Jeremiah 23:30 and 36 says, "Therefore, behold, I am against the prophets, saith the LORD, that steal my words every one from his neighbour. And the burden of the LORD shall ye mention no more: for every man's word shall be his burden; for ye have perverted the words of the living God, of the LORD of hosts our God."

The translation that has maintained the original Word of God is the King James Version Bible. Of course, there are objections to studying the KJV Bible, one of which is that it was written in AD 1611 and is difficult to read with its old English text. I have been reading the King James Bible for more than thirty years, and I have no problem understanding Scripture. When giving Bible studies or teaching a class, I have discovered that, in some cases, it is hard to prove sound doctrine using other Bibles even though people like them because they are supposedly easier to understand.

Some Bibles explain the meaning of Scripture— these versions are paraphrases and are the words and thoughts of men and women, not the words of God. The work of understanding Scripture is to be accomplished by asking God for wisdom, allowing the Holy Spirit to guide, and then applying God's principles to understand truth. This approach puts us on safe ground.

The following scriptures speak to the importance of studying the Bible:

- "Prove all things; hold fast that which is good" (1 Thess. 5:21).

- "Whom shall he teach knowledge? and whom shall he make to understand doctrine? them that are weaned from the milk, and drawn from the breasts. For precept must be upon precept, precept upon precept; line upon line; line upon line; here a little, and there a little" (Isa. 28:9–10).

- "Which things also we speak, not in the words which man's wisdom teacheth, but which the Holy Ghost teacheth; comparing spiritual things with spiritual" (1 Cor. 2:13).

- "These were more noble than those in Thessalonica, in that they received the word with all readiness of mind, and searched the scriptures daily, whether those things were so" (Acts 17:11).

We must study the Bible for ourselves to ensure that we are on the straight and narrow path leading to heaven. The following Scripture warns us to put our trust in God's Word: "It is better to trust in the LORD than to put confidence in man" (Ps. 118:8). There are so many Christian churches that believe differently from each other, and yet Jesus prayed for unity among the brethren while He was with His disciples (John 17). The Bible warns us to watch and be ready, shunning darkness and embracing light—"And have no fellowship with the unfruitful works of darkness, but rather reprove them" (Eph. 5:11).

Romans 1:25 speaks about the dangers of changing God's Word: "Who changed the truth of God into a lie, and worshipped and served the creature more than the Creator, who is blessed forever. Amen."

In Matthew 15:3 and 9 it is written: "Why do ye also transgress the commandment of God by your tradition?… But in vain they do worship me, teaching for doctrines the commandments of men."

Satan is working twenty-four hours a day, seven days a week to try to confuse us and weaken the power of God's Word. God warns us to be wise and follow Him no matter what: "See then that ye walk circumspectly, not as fools, but as wise, redeeming the time, because the days are evil. Wherefore be ye not unwise, but understanding what the will of the Lord is" (Eph. 5:15–17).

Chapter 5

God's Pure, Preserved, and Unadulterated Word

L est we become discouraged, we have the assurance that God is in control and has won the battle against Satan. God's Word has been preserved throughout the ages to give us comfort and guidance. The Bible is the pure Word of God, given to His people to guide them until the second coming of Jesus.

We serve a powerful God who is in charge of all things. King Solomon wrote, "I know that, whatsoever God doeth, it shall be for ever: nothing can be put to it, nor any thing taken from it: and God doeth it, that men should fear before him" (Eccl. 3:14). Paul wrote to the church in Thessalonica: "For this cause also thank we God without ceasing, because, when ye received the word of God which ye heard of us, ye received it not as the word of men, but as it is in truth, the word of God, which effectually worketh also in you that believe" (1 Thess. 2:13).

Standing Fast in the Truth

God's true followers will stand fast for the truth as it is in Jesus. But we must be watchful as Jesus warned

His disciples to be: "Take heed lest any man deceive you" (Mark 13:5).

Because we have confidence in the pure Word of God, we can detect a false shepherd, a false Bible, or erroneous Scripture. All Scripture is truth (John 17:17). Therefore, if we detect perverted Scripture not in harmony with the rest of the Bible or if it does not correctly represent Jesus, we must run from that Bible translation because it cannot be trusted to prepare us for eternal life with God. As we study the Bible, we must pray and ask God for wisdom. The Holy Spirit is your Guide; He will help you make important decisions. "Howbeit when he, the Spirit of truth, is come, he will guide you into all truth: for he shall not speak of himself; but whatsoever he shall hear, that shall he speak: and he will shew you things to come" (John 16:13).

Jesus told His disciples, "My sheep hear my voice, and I know them, and they follow me" (John 10:27). God's Word reveals His standard for life. It is His love letter to humankind. "The words of the LORD are pure words... Thou shalt keep them, O LORD, thou shalt preserve them from this generation for ever" (Ps. 12:6–7). "For ever, O LORD, thy word is settled in heaven" (Ps. 119:89).

While on earth, Jesus promised His disciples that "heaven and earth shall pass away, but my words shall not pass away" (Matt. 24:35). After His death and resurrection, the apostles confirmed the lasting power of God's Word: "Being born again ... by the word of God, which liveth and abideth for ever.... But the word of the Lord endureth for ever" (1 Peter 1:23, 25). All of these passages of scripture point to a true, living, pure Bible.

God's Faithful Christian Believers Are Prepared for Eternity Through His Word

There are many different Christian churches in the world—Catholics, Baptists, Lutherans, Seventh-day Adventists, Methodists, Jehovah's Witnesses, Presbyterians, Episcopalians, etc. So which church should we belong to? Although God's Word does not mention any of today's de- nominations by name, the Bible does identify His church: "But if I tarry long, that thou mayest know how thou oughtest to behave thyself in the house of God, which is the church of the living God, the pillar and ground of the truth" (1 Tim. 3:15).

We must be able to trust our Bible because its truth identifies which church God wants us to belong to. Here is another identifying truth of God's church: "Here is the patience of the saints: here are they that keep the commandments of God, and the faith of Jesus" (Rev. 14:12). Does your church believe and teach the keeping of all the Ten Commandments of the moral law, including "Remember the Sabbath day to keep it holy" (Exod. 20:8)? James under inspiration of God says: "For whosoever shall keep the whole law, and yet offend in one point, he is guilty of all" (James 2:10). What is known sinning? "Whosoever committeth sin transgresseth also the law: for sin is the transgression of the law" (1 John 3:4). God assures us in the New Testament that He will put His laws in our heart. Paul says this about God: "This is the covenant that I will make with them after those days, saith the Lord, I will put my laws into their hearts, and in their minds will I write them" (Heb. 10:16). Read also Psalm 19:7–11; Revelation 22:14; Matthew 1:21. God assures us that He will put them in our hearts (see Heb. 8:10).

As earth's history draws to a close, God's faithful people will trust Him, love the truth, and make a stand to preserve the Word of God. We must remember to trust and believe God with all our heart at all times: "Trust in the LORD with all thine heart; and lean not unto thine own understanding" (Prov. 3:5).

Through faithfulness to God's Word, we will be ready for Christ's soon return. "And the very God of peace sanctify you wholly; and I pray God your whole spirit and soul and body be preserved blameless unto the coming of our Lord Jesus Christ. Faithful is he that calleth you, who also will do it" (1 Thess. 5:23–24).

Not only must we be faithful, but we must also love the truth: "And with all deceivableness of unrighteousness in them that perish; because they received not the love of the truth, that they might be saved" (2 Thess. 2:10). The reverse is also true. If we love the truth, we won't be deceived. God describes His people in the last days before Jesus' second coming: "Here is the patience of the saints: here are they that keep the commandments of God, and the faith of Jesus" (Rev. 14:12). "Blessed are they that do his commandments, that they may have right to the tree of life, and may enter in through the gates into the city" (Rev. 22:14). Oh, how we need to stay close to Jesus and His truths in God's Word. Read also John 15:1–5 and Philippians 4:13.

The Truth Protects Us

The true and trusted Word of God is our armor of protection and a light to our path. As we walk the Christian walk, we can stand strong knowing that the truth protects us. Paul provides us with the following description about the armor of God:

> Finally, my brethren, be strong in the Lord, and in the power of his might. Put on the whole armour of God, that ye may be able to stand against the wiles of the devil. For we wrestle not against flesh and blood, but against principalities, against powers, against the rulers of darkness of this world, against spiritual wickedness in high places. Wherefore take unto you the whole armour of God, that ye may be able to withstand in the evil day, and having done all, to stand. Stand therefore, having your loins girt about with truth, and having on the breastplate of righteousness; And your feet shod with the preparation of the gospel of peace; Above all, taking the shield of faith, wherewith ye shall be able to quench all the fiery darts of the wicked. And take on the helmet of salvation, and the sword of the Spirit, which is the word of God. (Eph. 6:10–17)

Our armor cannot be defective if we are to fight the devil and win the battle! If we are told to put on "the whole armour of God" then we must follow the whole Bible. But how can we do this if hundreds of words have been taken out or changed to give a different meaning to Scripture? We will look at the evidence later in our study regarding the changes that have taken place. For now, we are setting the stage, building a foundation, so the evidence will be clear and Satan's deceptions will be unmasked. King David wrote, "Thy word is a lamp unto my feet, and a light unto my path" (Ps. 119:105). As we walk in the light, we shall have life. "Then spake Jesus again unto them, saying, I am the light of the world: he that followeth me shall not walk in darkness, but shall have the light of life" (John 8:12).

I want to have a mind like Jesus (see Phil. 2:5). I want to develop His faith (see Rev. 14:12). And I want to develop His character in my life. God's Word tells us how we can do that: "Now the Lord is that Spirit: and where the Spirit of the Lord is, there is liberty. But we all, with open face beholding as in a glass the glory of the Lord, are changed into the same image from glory to glory, even as by the Spirit of the Lord" (2 Cor. 3:17–18). God is teaching me; He is teaching you. The more time we spend in God's Word, the more we will reflect His character. Please don't let the things of this world—TV, hobbies, sports, work, etc.—keep you from spending precious time reading God's Word each day. We can all benefit from being more like Christ.

Spiritual Food

We all know how important it is to eat physical food. (I eat at least twice a day.) In fact, Jesus mentioned physical food in the Lord's Prayer: "Give us this day our daily bread" (Matt. 6:11). But God also talks about our need for daily spiritual food: "It is written, That man shall not live by bread alone, but by *every word of God*" (Luke 4:4, emphasis added; see also Matt. 4:4). We are reminded to live by *every word of God*. Therefore, God is reminding us to be careful of omissions from the Bible, words missing that would water down the truth or change its meaning.

Having Confidence and Trusting in the Word of God

I have personally experienced the power of God's Word in my life. I know firsthand that our self-centered sinful minds can experience forgiveness and power from God. I know that we can become spiritual Christians with the full assurance of salvation. Reading the Bible and getting to know Jesus makes us want to be more like Him.

You and I can have confidence in God's Word because He gives it to all of us for our instruction. "Knowing this first, that no prophecy of scripture is of any private interpretation. For the prophecy came not in old time by the will of man: but holy men of God spake as they were moved by the Holy Ghost" (2 Peter 1:20—21). The Bible says, and I believe, that the words of Scripture are directly from God—they are God's words. "Every word of God is pure: he is a shield unto them that put their trust in him" (Prov. 30:5). Read also 1 Thessalonians 2:13: "For this cause also thank we God without ceasing, because, when ye received the word of God which ye heard of us, ye received it not as the word of men, but as it is in truth, the word of God, which effectually worketh also in you that believe."

If we do not believe in the Bible, we are calling God a liar: "He that believeth not God hath made him a liar; because he believeth not the record that God gave of his Son" (1 John 5:10).

God's Warning to His People

I believe that after reading the above scriptures and passages, God is warning us that any Bible that contains erroneous Scripture or missing Scriptures does not qualify as being the pure, unadulterated Word of God, and it cannot be trusted to lead us toward the kingdom. Why is there so much confusion about doctrine in so many Christian churches when the Bible clearly states that Jesus is "the way, the truth, and the life" (John 14:6)? Paul tells us that there is "one Lord, one faith, one baptism" (Eph. 4:5). If that is the case, why are there so many denominations?

I believe the answer lies in the wide variety of Bible translations, some that are filled with errors. The only way we can discern between truth and error is by using the Word of God. The only way we can know the difference between a true pastor or a false pastor, a true teacher or a false teacher, true doctrine or false doctrine, or a true church or a false church is by prayerfully studying the Bible. It is then that we will know the truth!

God will protect His flock if they trust in His Word. He has warned us in His Word to watch for false teachings: "Now I beseech you, brethren, mark them which cause divisions and offences contrary to the doctrine which ye have learned; and avoid them" (Rom. 16:17). Another warning is found in Isaiah 8:20: "To the law and to the testimony: if they speak not according to this word, it is because there is no light in them." So as not to be misunderstood, historically speaking, I believe that the King James Bible has been preserved from the original manuscripts of the inspired Word of God. God gave us His best when He gave us Jesus as our Savior. Only God Himself is absolutely infallible or perfect in the highest sense, but from more than two years of research, I believe the King James Bible is the best Bible translation that represents Jesus Christ, the Word of God (see John 1:1–3, 14) for God's English-speaking people. Bibles in other languages are good and faithful if they also trace their beginnings from the Received Text.

CHAPTER 6

God Is Not the Author of Confusion

As we continue this study, I want to present principles from the Bible that speak to God's character. "God is not the author of confusion, but of peace, as in all churches of the saints" (1 Cor. 14:33). The Bible also says that God cannot lie. "In hope of eternal life, which God, that cannot lie, promised before the world began" (Titus 1:2). Jesus said, "Sanctify them through thy truth: thy word is truth" (John 17:17).

My point is that if confusion exists, if error exists, we are reading the wrong Bible translation! In the same way that "God is not the author of confusion," He wants His followers to be like Him and clearly speak the truth. "Now I beseech you, brethren, by the name of our Lord Jesus Christ, that ye all speak the same thing, and that there be no divisions among you; but that ye be perfectly joined together in the same mind and in the same judgment" (1 Cor. 1:10). My question is this: How can we have the same mind if we are reading different Bibles that teach different things, different doctrines? We just learned that God is not the author of confusion, but it is confusing when you are reading the King James Bible, and the pastor is preaching from a different Bible that doesn't say the same thing. When having Bible studies, I have found that the King James Version gets straight to the point in teaching Bible truths and doctrines. When using other modern translations, a lot of proof texts are no longer black and white but now fall into gray areas, causing many people to fall into the trap of private interpretation.

CHAPTER 7

Can the King James Version Bible Be Understood?

Although some individuals question whether the King James Version Bible can be understood or not, God has made it clear through Scripture that if we seek Him, we will find Him: "The entrance of thy words giveth light; it giveth understanding unto the simple" (Ps. 119:130). According to this scripture, you don't have to have a college degree to understand God's Holy Word. He says He gives understanding to the "simple." Children as well as full-grown adults can understand it. God promises to gives us help if we need it.

Modern translations such as the New International Version, Revised Standard Version, New English Bible, Good News Bible, Today's English Version, etc., are promoted as being easier to understand with their use of modern English. Sounds good, right? Not so fast! Within some of these new versions, Scriptures are not the same. Doctrine becomes confusing and harder to prove. Chapter 9 will outline the differences between the various translations.

Our understanding of Scripture is based on our relationship with Christ. In 1 Corinthians 2:14, it says that "the natural man receiveth not the things of the Spirit of God: for they are foolishness unto him: neither can he know them, because they are spiritually discerned." If Scripture seems to be difficult, we should pray and ask God for wisdom. He will give us extra help through the Holy Spirit, our heavenly Counselor. "Then opened he their understanding, that they might understand the scriptures" (Luke 24:45).

Jesus said we must come to God like a child: "Verily I say unto you, Whosoever shall not receive the kingdom of God as a little child, he shall not enter therein" (Mark 10:15). When Enoch had his first child, he recognized this important fact and walked with God. God was so pleased that He took Enoch to heaven without seeing death (see Gen. 5:22–24). God is our Creator. He knows what is best for us. Like Enoch, we must have the simplicity and faith of a little child. We must be willing to learn and to ask the Holy Spirit to give us understanding and wisdom. When we think of God and His greatness, may we humbly open His Word with godly fear and reverence. May we always ask God, "How can I apply these things I am learning to my life?"

If we are struggling to understand Bible truths, we can call upon the name of Jesus and He will send us the Comforter and Counselor: "Howbeit when he, the Spirit of truth, is come, he will guide you into all truth" (John 16:13).

As we have discussed, the requirement for receiving understanding from God's Word is simple—all we have to do is prayerfully ask for God's guidance. The next two passages of Scripture show us how to gain understanding: "Then shall ye call upon me, and ye shall go and pray unto me, and I will hearken unto you. And ye shall seek me, and find me, when ye shall search for me with all your heart" (Jer. 29:12–13). "Yea, if thou criest after knowledge, and liftest up thy voice for understanding; If thou seekest her as silver, and searchest for her as for hid treasures; Then shalt thou understand the fear of the LORD, and find the knowledge of God. For the LORD giveth wisdom: out of his mouth cometh knowledge and understanding" (Prov. 2:3–6).

Food for thought: People will tell you that the English language is one of the hardest to learn, yet it comes easily to children who grow up with it. At my age (sixty-five years mature), learning to use the computer has been very hard. It took much prayer and asking God for wisdom to be able to write this book. I would press wrong buttons and lose many hours of work, or it would freeze up, and I wouldn't know what to do. Children, however, grow up on the computer, and they are very skilled at using it. My point is that we should want to read God's preserved and faithful Bible, and this chapter explains how we can understand it! Just because a Bible is supposedly easier to understand is not the *best* reason for choosing it to prepare us for eternity. Modern English translations can be good reference Bibles. Some words may be easier to understand, but it is important to compare them to the King James Bible to prevent a possible watering down of the truth.

CHAPTER 8

Beware of Satan's Deceptions

Because Satan knows his time is short, he is working overtime to deceive as many people as possible (see Rev. 12:12). As I have studied and compared different Bibles, I believe one of Satan's greatest attacks at this time is on the Word of God. He knows it is our only defense against him, so he has set out to cause confusion with the Bible. May we never underestimate his power or deceptions.

Our spiritual warfare weapon against Satan *must* be reliable. We must be able to stand on the truths of the Bible. Paul says it like this: "(For the weapons of our warfare are not carnal, but mighty through God to the pulling down of strong holds;) Casting down imaginations, and every high thing that exalteth itself against the knowledge of God, and bringing into captivity every thought to the obedience of Christ" (2 Cor. 10:4–5).

Beware of the Devil

The Bible warns us about Satan's lies and deceptions. Following are four texts from the New Testament that remind us to be watchful:

- "Beware of false prophets, which come to you in sheep's clothing, but inwardly they are ravening wolves" (Matt. 7:15).

- "Ye are of your father the devil, and the lusts of your father ye will do. He was a murderer from the beginning, and abode not in the truth, because there is no truth in him. When he speaketh a lie, he speaketh of his own: for he is a liar, and the father of it" (John 8:44).

- "And no marvel; for Satan himself is transformed into an angel of light. Therefore it is no great thing if his ministers also be transformed as ministers of righteousness; whose end shall be according to their works" (2 Cor. 11:14–15).

- "Be sober, be vigilant; because your adversary the devil, as a roaring lion, walketh about, seeking whom he may devour" (1 Peter 5:8).

God's sincere elect, His remnant people who "keep the commandments of God" (Rev. 14:12), have only one thing to protect themselves against Satan's devices— the pure, unadulterated Word of God. Everything is measured against "thus sayeth the Lord." Like Simon Peter, we must recognize that the Bible possesses the words of eternal life: "Lord, to whom shall we go? thou hast the words of eternal life. And we believe and are sure that thou art that Christ, the Son of the living God" (John 6:68–69).

If we want to be safe, we must hide God's Word in our hearts. David says it like this: "Wherewithal shall a young man cleanse his way? by taking heed thereto according to thy word.... Thy word have I hid in mine heart, that I might not sin against thee" (Ps. 119:9, 11).

God's Plan and Satan's Attempt to Trap Us

God has given us a map, a blueprint, a guide, if you please, to show us the plan of salvation. God's Word is meant to encourage us to put on the mind of Christ (see Phil. 2:5), develop "the faith of Jesus" (Rev. 14:12), and prepare us to spend eternity with God. However, "the god of this world hath blinded the minds of them which believe not" (2 Cor. 4:4). Even Christians who go to church, if they don't read their Bible to know God's will for their lives, can be easily deceived. Satan has been working hard; false Christs, false prophets, false teachers, and even questionable Bible translations have arisen to trick Christ's followers: "If it were possible, they shall deceive the very elect" (Matt. 24:24).

As long as we are connected to Christ and have hidden His Word in our hearts, we will defeat the attacks of Satan. Jesus encouraged His disciples and warned them to "take heed to yourselves, lest at any time your hearts be overcharged with surfeiting, and drunkenness, and cares of this life, and so that day come upon you unawares. For as a snare shall it come on all them that dwell on the face of the whole earth. Watch ye therefore, and pray always, that ye may be accounted worthy to escape all these things that shall come to pass, and to stand before the Son of man" (Luke 21:34–36).

The devil's job is to make sure we are lost. Christ's job is to make sure we are saved. In this busy world we live in, who is on the throne of your heart, self or Jesus? Our choice determines our destiny! From reading the above scriptures, I believe Satan is trying to ensnare us.

Too much TV, sports, hobbies, work, self can crowd out God and can become our gods if we don't have time to read His Word. The wrong Bible could also ensnare us. I'll let you decide.

In the next chapter, we are going to compare the King James Version Bible with other popular translations that can be found in many Christian churches. Hold on to your seat; you may be amazed and shocked like I was. Please ask the Holy Spirit to help you maintain an open mind before determining the validity of this study.

CHAPTER 9

The Facts: A Comparison of Bible Translations

This chapter will present a number of passages from the King James Version Bible and demonstrate how the verses are changed or omitted in other translations. As a result of these changes, our faith is weakened, causing confusion and, in some cases, even changing sound doctrine. Doctrine is important; Paul says so in 2 Timothy 4:1–8.

Salvation

Text: "For God so loved the world, that he gave his only begotten Son, that whosoever believeth in him should not perish, but have everlasting life" (John 3:16).

Comparison: "Only begotten Son" has been taken out of other modern Bible translations. For example, the New International Version says: "For God so loved the world that he gave his one and only Son, that whoever believes in him shall not perish but have eternal life." Another popular paraphrase, The Living Bible, writes: "For God loved the world so much that he gave his only Son so that anyone who believes in him shall not perish but have everlasting life." Check your particular translation.

- Good News Bible/Today's English Version
- New English Bible
- J.B. Phillips New Testament in Modern English
- Revised Standard Version

Comments: God has only one "only begotten Son" (Mic. 5:2; Prov. 8:22–30), but He has many other sons. "Now there was a day when the sons of God came to present themselves before the LORD, and Satan came also among them" (Job 1:6). Believers are adopted sons. "But as many as receive him, to them gave he power to become the sons of God, even to them that believe on his name" (John 1:12). So, a distinct difference must be made to show the significance of Christ's sacrifice as God's "only begotten Son."

Text: "For I am not ashamed of the gospel of Christ: for it is the power of God unto salvation to every one that believeth; to the Jew first, and also to the Greek" (Rom. 1:16).

Comparison: The "gospel of Christ" has been taken out in the following translations:

- American Standard Bible
- Good News Bible/ Today's English Version
- New English Bible
- New International Version
- Revised Standard Version

Comments: Paul warned of another perverted gospel being taught. Read Galatians 1:8–9. May we only listen to and obey "the gospel of Christ," which was faithfully written in the King James Version.

Text: "Forasmuch then as Christ hath suffered for us in the flesh, arm yourselves likewise with the same mind: for he that hath suffered in the flesh hath ceased from sin" (1 Peter 4:1).

Comparison: Other modern translations leave out the part that Christ suffered "for us." This is what the Revised Standard Version says: "Since therefore Christ suffered in the flesh, arm yourselves with the same thought, for whoever has suffered in the flesh has ceased from sin." If you are not reading the King James Version, check your translation to see what it says.

Comments: Why did Christ suffer? It is very important for us to know that He suffered for us and that salvation is a reality in our life if we accept His grace, which is freely offered to us. Thus, we can become Christians. Please read Isaiah 53:5 and 1 Peter 2:24–25.

Text: "But if ye do not forgive, neither will your Father which is in heaven forgive your trespasses" (Mark 11:26).

Comparison: This whole scripture has been taken out of the following Bible translations:

- New International Version
- Revised Standard Version

Text: "For the Son of man is come to save that which was lost" (Matt. 18:11).

Comparison: Again, this whole scripture is omitted in the following translations:

- Contemporary English Version
- New English Bible

- New International Version
- New Revised Standard Version

Text: "And Philip said, If thou believest with all thine heart, thou mayest. And he answered and said, I believe that Jesus Christ is the Son of God" (Acts 8:37).

Comparison: In the King James Version, this is one of my favorite scriptures. It is a very important scripture. But this entire scripture has been omitted in many other modern Bibles:

- Good News Bible/ Today's English Version
- Jerusalem Bible
- New International Version
- New World Translation of the Holy Scriptures
- Revised Standard Version

Comments: Even the demons believe that Jesus Christ is the Son of God (see Mark 5:2–9; Matt. 8:28–29). However, their head knowledge cannot save them. As the King James Version Bible upholds, we must believe in our heart that we are saved, and we shall be saved (see Jer. 24:7; Ps. 15:2; Rom. 10:9–10; Heb. 10:38–39).

A great evangelist I knew personally, Joe Crews, once said: "There is twelve inches between heaven and hell, the distance between the head and the heart." That statement left quite an impression on me!

Text: "For in Christ Jesus neither circumcision availeth any thing, nor uncircumcision, but a new creature. And as many as walk according to this rule, peace be on them, and mercy, and upon the Israel of God" (Gal. 6:15–16).

Comparison: The phrase "for in Christ Jesus" is omitted in most translations. Check your particular Bible. For example, the New International Version says, "Neither circumcision nor uncircumcision means anything; what counts is a new creation. Peace and mercy to all who follow this rule—to the Israel of God."

Comments: As Bible-believing Christians (see Matt. 4:4), we no longer look toward physical Israel; we believe in spiritual Israel (see Gal. 3:26–29; Rom. 2:28–29; 9:6–8).

God's people are born-again Christians (see 2 Cor. 5:17)—spiritual Israel. Why settle for half of the truth, when the King James Version gives you the whole truth of this particular scripture?

Text: "And Jesus answered him, saying, It is written, That man shall not live by bread alone, but by every word of God" (Luke 4:4).

Comparison: The phrase "but by every word of God" has been omitted, taken out of other translations. Beware! For example, in the Good News Bible, it is written, "But Jesus answered, 'The scripture says, "Human beings cannot live on bread alone."'"

Comments: So, what are we supposed to live by. By reading the whole verse, God is reminding us that we need spiritual food to survive spiritually. The other translations omit the most important part of this scripture. "Every word" means that if one word is taken away it leaves the Bible incomplete. Hundreds of words have been taken out of the modern translations of the Bible. The Lord is clear about how He feels regarding the desecration of His Word: "Therefore, behold, I am against the prophets, saith the Lord, that steal my words every one from his neighbour" (Jer. 23:30).

Repentance

Text: "When Jesus heard it, he saith unto them, They that are whole have no need of the physician, but they that are sick: I came not to call the righteous, but sinners to repentance" (Mark 2:17).

Comparison: The phrase "to repentance" is omitted. For example, the verse reads as follows in the Revised Standard Version: "And when Jesus heard it, he said to them, 'Those who are well have no need of a physician, but those who are sick; I came not to call the righteous, but sinners." These other translations have omitted the phrase:

- Good News Bible/ Today's English Version
- New English Bible
- New International Version
- New World Translation of the Holy Scriptures
- J.B. Phillips New Testament in Modern English

Comments: I take no pleasure in pointing out these omissions in Scripture. I only want to unmask Satan's deceptions. The absolute truth is that without repentance there is no salvation. I believe Bible translations that leave out the word repentance reinforce the false doctrine of salvation in sin. We don't need a false assurance of salvation. Read 2 Chronicles 15:2 and Matthew 24:13.

Text: "But go ye and learn what that meaneth, I will have mercy, and not sacrifice: for I am not come to call the righteous, but sinners to repentance" (Matt. 9:13).

Comparison: Once again, the phrase "to repentance" is omitted in many Bible translations. Check your particular Bible. For example, the New International Version says, "But go and learn what this means, 'I desire mercy, not sacrifice.' For I have not come to call the righteous, but sinners."

Comments: The influence of an incomplete Bible could make an incomplete or deceived Christian. This book was written to minimize that possibility. Following are a couple thoughts about the importance of repentance. Repentance must precede forgiveness, for it is only "a broken and contrite heart" that is acceptable to God (Ps. 51:17; please read the whole chapter). Repentance includes sorrow for sin and a turning away from it. Why? Because sin separates us from God (see Isa. 59:2). Jesus came to save us from our sins, not in our sins (see Matt. 1:21). Calvary motivates us to hate sin.

The Christian's response: But he [Jesus] was wounded for our transgressions, he was bruised for our iniquities: the chastisement of our peace was upon him; and with his stripes <u>we are healed</u>" (Isa. 53:5). Read also 1 Peter 2:24–25 and 2 Corinthians 5:21. We are to hate sin the way God hates sin: "And God saw that the wickedness of man was great in the earth, and that every imagination of the thoughts of his heart was only evil continually. And it repented the Lord that he had made man on the earth, and it grieved him at his heart" (Gen. 6:5–6). Read also Exodus 32:1–10 and Ezekiel 33:11. Grace with a warning: Isaiah 59:1–2.

The Plan of Salvation in the Old Testament

Text: "Thy way, O God, is in the sanctuary: who is so great a God as our God?" (Ps. 77:13).

Comparison: The phrase "is in the sanctuary" is omitted in a number of modern versions of the Bible. For example, in the Good News Bible it says, "Your ways, God, are holy. What god is so great as our God?" These other translations do not contain the phrase:

- New International Version
- Revised Standard Version

Comments: To better understand the plan of salvation in the New Testament, we should also study the sanctuary in the Old Testament. Both concepts point to God's grace— one looks forward to the cross, and the other looks back at the cross. Titus 2:11–12 says, "For the grace of God that bringeth salvation hath appeared to <u>all men</u>, Teaching us that, denying ungodliness and worldly lusts, we should live soberly, righteously, and godly, <u>in this present world</u>."

The devil doesn't want us to fully understand these things because he knows his power will be broken and he will be defeated if people read God's Word, understand it, and pledge their allegiance to the Son of God. (Read 1 John 3:8.)

The Hope of Eternal Life

Text: "Laying up in store for themselves a good foundation against the time to come, that they may lay hold on eternal life" (1 Tim. 6:19).

Comparison: The phrase "eternal life" is omitted in the Revised Standard Version. Instead, it says, "Thus laying up for themselves a good foundation for the future, so that they may take hold of the life that is life indeed." Other modern translations that have also omitted eternal life are:

- Good News Bible/Today's English Version
- New English Bible
- New International Version
- New World Translation of the Holy Scriptures
- Revised Standard Version

Comments: Having a personal relationship with Jesus Christ can give us a good life according to most Bible translations. However, the original verse in the King James Version promises us more than just a good life. We are told that we can have eternal life.

Satan

Text: "And Jesus answered and said unto him, Get thee behind me, Satan: for it is written, Thou shalt worship the Lord thy God, and him only shalt thou serve" (Luke 4:8).

Comparison: "Get behind me, Satan" has been omitted from other modern version Bibles. Was it an oversight? I believe this is one of the many examples of Satan tampering with God's Word to weaken its powerful influence! This is what the Good News Bible says: "Jesus answered, The scripture says, 'Worship the Lord your God and serve only him!'" Check your translation and these to see what it says.

- Good News Bible/ Today's English Version
- The Living Bible (which is not a translation of God's Word but a paraphrase)
- New International Version
- New World Translation of the Holy Scriptures
- Revised Standard Version

Comment: When we are strong in Jesus, we can say "get behind me, Satan." James wrote, "Submit yourselves therefore to God. Resist the devil, and he will flee from you" (James 4:7). That's the only way we can truly worship and serve God. It was no accident that the words were omitted in Luke 4:8. We need to run away from Bibles that weaken the truth of God's Word.

Slave of Satan or Servant of God?

Text: "Being then made free from sin, ye became the servants of righteousness." (Romans 6:18)

Comparison: In the New International Version the same Scripture says, "You have been set free from sin and have become slaves to righteousness."

The word "servant" was also changed to "slave" in:

- The Living Bible (a paraphrase Bible)
- Good News Bible/Today's English Version
- Revised Standard Version
- New King James Version

Comment: A servant *makes the choice* to obey God from the heart. Read Ephesians 6:6. A slave has *no choice*, they are held in bondage. Jesus does not force us to obey God, we choose to obey because of love! "If ye love me, keep my commandments" (John 14:15), in Christ's strength (see Phil 4:13 and Jude 24).

Trinity—The Union of God the Father, His Only Begotten Son (Jesus), and The Holy Spirit—All three, Doing Their Part Relating to Mankind's Salvation, read (Matthew 28:19; 2 Corinthians

13:14). Text: "For there are three that bear record in heaven, the Father, the Word, and the Holy Ghost: and these three are one" (1 John 5:7). God unites all three: "One God and Father of all, who is above all, and through all, and in you all" (Eph. 4:6).

Comparison: In 1 John 5:7, the phrase "the Father, the Word, and the Holy Ghost" is omitted in other Bible translations. For example, the New International Version says, "For there are three that testify." If you don't have a King James Version, check your modern Bible translation. The following versions omit the phrase:

- Good News Bible/Today's English Version
- The Living Bible totally omits 1 John 5:7, 8
- New World Translation of the Holy Scriptures
- Revised Standard Version

Comments: What three? Many other Bible translations do not specify who is being spoken about. One God or three Gods? Paul, under inspiration of God, says this: "But to us there is but *one God*, the Father, of whom are all things, and we by him; and one Lord Jesus Christ, by whom are all things, and we by him" (1 Cor. 8:6; John 17:3). The Holy Spirit is "The Spirit of God" (Rom. 8:9). "The Spirit of Jesus" in us (Gal. 4:6). Remember—God and Jesus are in heaven but the Holy Spirit is down here on planet earth with God's people, the Brethren (John 14:16, 17; Matt. 28:20; John 16:8).

The Blood of Jesus

Text: "In whom we have redemption through his blood, even the forgiveness of sins" (Col. 1:14).

Comparison: The phrase "through his blood" is omitted. For example, the New International Version says, "In whom we have redemption, the forgiveness of sins." The following translations do not contain the phrase:

- Good News Bible/ Today's English Version
- New English Bible
- Revised Standard Bible

Comments: Satan wants the phrase "through his blood" omitted because it is Christ's blood that saves us and covers us. I thank God for the faithfulness of the King James Version. If you are questioning the importance of the blood, read 1 Peter 1:18–19.

Peter is the Rock Versus Jesus is the Rock

Text: "And I say also unto thee, That thou art Peter, and upon this rock I will build my church; and the gates of hell shall not prevail against it" (Matt. 16:18).

Comparison: Catholics believe that Peter is the rock of the church and the foundation they are built on. This belief is upheld in some modern version Bibles that come from original Catholic manuscripts—Sinaiticus and Vaticanus, and the Latin Vulgate Bible. Different from the King James Version manuscript, the Received Text is the only one that was not influenced by the Catholic Church. Now you know why all Bibles do not teach the same doctrine. Unless brought to their attention, most Christians are not aware of these facts.

The following translations point to Peter as *the* rock:

- Good News Bible/Today's English Version also says:

- "And so I tell you, Peter: you are <u>a rock,</u> and on <u>this rock foundation</u> I will build my church, and not even death will ever be able to overcome it."

- J.B. Phillips New Testament in Modern English: "Now I tell you that you are Peter <u>the rock</u>, and it is on this rock that I am going to found my Church, and the powers of death will never prevail against it."

- New English Bible: "And I say this to you; you are Peter the Rock, and on this rock I will build my church, and the power of death shall never conquer it."

Comments: As Bible-believing Christians who compare scripture with scripture (see Isa. 28:9–10; 1 Cor. 2:13), if we let the Bible teach us, we will clearly see that Jesus is the Rock, not Peter (1 Cor. 10:4; Ps. 62:2, 6). Jesus is the Chief Cornerstone of the church (see Eph. 2:20). Again, we can thank God for the faithfulness of the King James Version.

Faults Verses Sins

Text: "Confess your faults one to another, and pray one for another, that ye may be healed. The effectual fervent prayer of a righteous man availeth much" (James 5:16).

Comparison: A fault is something that is not as it should be—a mistake, forgetting something, coming to a wrong conclusion—not deliberately sinning against God. Sin is open rebellion against God, breaking one of God's moral Ten Commandment laws (see 1 John 3:4).

The same scripture in the New International Version says, "Therefore confess your sins to each other and pray for each other so that you may be healed. The prayer of a righteous person is powerful and effective." Check your own Bible translation. The following translations change the above verse:

- Good News Bible/Today's English Version
- J.B. Phillips New Testament in Modern English
- New English Bible
- Revised Standard Version

Comments: We confess our faults to one another. We confess our sins to God (see Micah 7:18–19; 1 John 1:9) through Jesus Christ: "For there is one God, and one mediator between God and men, the man Christ Jesus" (1 Tim. 2:5). Confessing our sins to a priest in the confessional is upheld in modern versions by changing "faults" to "sins." These are two very different words that present very different meanings.

Text: "For which things' sake the wrath of God cometh on the children of disobedience" (Col. 3:6).

Comparison: The phrase "on the children of disobedience" is omitted in the New International Version and the Revised Standard Version. The NIV reads: "Because of these, the wrath of God is coming," and the RSV reads: "On account of these the wrath of God is coming."

Comments: "The gospel of Christ" gives people the power to stop rebelling against God (see Rom. 1:16). This is salvation from sin. If we continue to rebel in disobedience to God, it only proves that we don't believe that God took the Ten Commandments off the tables of stone and put them in our hearts. "For this is the covenant that I will make with the house of Israel after those days, saith the

Lord; I will put my laws into their mind, and write them in their hearts: and I will be to them a God, and they shall be to me a people" (Heb. 8:10).

If we lack faith, we can strengthen our faith by spending more time with Jesus, who is the Word of God (see Rom 10:17). If we want to be more Christ-like, again, we must spend more time reading God's Word (see 2 Cor. 3:17–18).

Victory Over Sin

Text: "There is therefore now no condemnation to them which are in Christ Jesus, who walk not after the flesh, but after the Spirit" (Rom. 8:1).

Comparison: The most important part of this scripture was omitted. For example, the New International Version states: "Therefore, there is now no condemnation for those who are in Christ Jesus." Many other modern version Bibles also omit the most important part of this scripture.

- Good News Bible/Today's English Version
- J.B. Phillips New Testament in Modern English
- The Living Bible
- New International Version
- New World Translation of the Holy Scriptures
- Revised Standard Version

Comments: Satan doesn't mind if we understand that we have "no condemnation in Christ Jesus," but he doesn't want us to know why. The answer is that by God's grace we are no longer sinning after the flesh but we are living victoriously in the Spirit. Praise God! Read Romans 8 and Galatians 5:16–21; 6:7–9.

The King James Version teaches the truth about forgiveness and the power to stop sinning. By omitting the last part of the verse, only half of the truth is presented, thus becoming a lie and promoting that we only have to believe in Jesus. There is no call to repentance or victory over sin. Read Jude 1:4 and 2 Peter 2:1–3, 14–15. The perverted gospel Paul warned about. Read also Galatians 1:6–7.

Text: "Blessed are they that do his commandments, that they may have right to the tree of life, and may enter in through the gates into the city" (Rev. 22:14).

Comparison: The New International Version says this in the same Scripture: "Blessed are those who wash their robes, that they may have right to the tree of life and may go through the gates into the city." Once again, the mention of "blessed are they that do his commandments" has been omitted in the following modern versions. Read for yourself.

- Today's English Version
- Revised Standard Version
- New English Bible, etc.

Comments: Jesus said, "If ye love me, keep my commandments" (John 14:15; see also verse 21). There is nothing legalistic about that! In Christ's strength we can do all things (Phil. 4:13). "The whole duty of man" is to keep His commandments (Eccles. 12:13, 14). We can't wash our own robes—only Jesus can! "In whom we have redemption through his blood, the forgiveness of sins, according to the riches of his grace" (Eph. 1:7).

Text: "Study to shew thyself approved unto God, a workman that needeth not to be ashamed, rightly dividing the word of truth." (2 Tim. 2:15).

Comparison: The important word "study" has been omitted (deleted) in other translations of the Bible. Example: In the New King James Bible it says: "Be diligent to present yourself approved to God, a worker who does not need to be ashamed, rightly dividing the word of truth." Other Bible translations that also have "study" missing in this Scripture:

- Revised Standard Version
- Good News Bible/Today's English Version
- Living Bible
- Phillips Modern English
- New English Bible
- New International Version

Comment: Other translations tell us to "do our best," "work hard," "try hard." Working our "hardest," and doing our "best" will not give us victory over Satan, we must "study" God's Word and put on Jesus as the King James Bible faithfully tells us to do in this Scripture!

Salvation in Sin: No Such Gospel!

Text: "We know that whosoever is born of God sinneth not; but he that is begotten of God keepeth himself, and the wicked one toucheth him not" (1 John 5:18).

Comparison: The Living Bible says, "No one who has become part of God's family makes a practice of sinning, for Christ, God's Son, holds him securely, and the devil cannot get his hands on him." Look at 1 John 3:9 in the same Bible: "The person who has been born into God's family does not make a practice of sinning because now God's life is in him; so he can't keep on sinning, for his new life has been born into and controls him—he has been *born again*."

Comment: "Practice sinning" is sinning on a regular basis, and Christians don't do that. Whether deliberate or not, The Living Bible implies they just willfully and knowingly sin less. I have heard pastors say, "It's not whether we sin or not, it's what direction we are going that determines our salvation." This scripture gives the impression that believers can't have victory over sin! We must believe in our heart (see Matt. 1:21) that Jesus will save us from—not in—our sins. He did not tell the woman caught in adultery to sin less; Jesus said, "Go, and sin no more" (John 8:11). Read also Philippians 4:13, 1 Corinthians 10:13, and Jude 24.

Text: "And he gave some, apostles; and some, prophets; and some, evangelists; and some, pastors and teachers; For the perfecting of the saints, for the work of the ministry, for the edifying of the body of Christ" (Eph. 4:11–12)

Comparison: Other translations omit (delete) "for the perfecting of the saints" Example: The New King James Bible says, "for the equipping of the saints" See what your translation says. Others that also omit these important words:

- Today's English Version/Good News Bible
- Living Bible
- Phillips Modern English
- Revised Standard Version
- New International Version

Comment: The Bible encourages us to get off the milk and get into the meat of God's Word. We are encouraged to grow up and be perfect (Greek–Mature Christians). Read Matthew 5:48. Other Translations say "special abilities," "to equip the saints." These words do notalways mean mature. Again, the King James Bible is faithful to the truth with no gray area to encourage "private interpretation."

Text: Blotting out the handwriting of ordinances that was against us, which was contrary to us, and took it out of the way, nailing it to his cross;... Let no man therefore judge you in meat, or in drink, or in respect of an holyday, or of a new moon, or of the sabbath days" (Col. 2:14, 16).

Comparison: For example, the Revised Standard Version says, "Having canceled the <u>bond</u> which stood against us with its <u>legal demands</u>; this he set aside, nailing it to the cross.... Therefore let no one pass judgment on you in questions of food and drink or with regard to a festival or a new moon or a sabbath."

The phrase "handwriting of ordinances" was omitted from the following translations, thus eliminating the difference between the Old Testament ordinances found in Leviticus 23 that led up to the cross and God's moral Ten Commandment law.

- American Standard Version
- Contemporary English Version
- Good News Bible/ Today's English Version
- New English Bible
- New International Bible
- New World Translation of the Holy Scriptures

Comments: The confusing words "bond" and "legal demands" open up this text for private interpretation.

By allowing ourselves to read these unclear scriptures, doubt creeps in as to what the truth is. The "ordinances that *was* against us" that were *nailed to the cross*—which included food, festival-type sabbaths, Old Testament priests, and animal sacrifices in the sanctuary services—must not be confused with God's moral Ten Commandments, which are not against us and which Paul said would be established forever (see Rom. 3:31).

The moral law is "perfect, converting the soul: the testimony of the Lord is sure, making wise the simple. More to be desired are they than gold, yea, than much fine gold: sweeter also than honey and the honeycomb" (Ps. 19:7, 10). "Wherefore the law is holy, and the commandment holy, and just, and good" (Rom. 7:12). How can it be "against us"? Which one of the Ten Commandments is okay for a Christian to break? Thou shalt not commit adultery? Remember the Sabbath day to keep it holy?

James wrote, "For whosoever shall keep the whole law, and yet offend in one point, he is guilty of all" (James 2:10). The beloved John said, "If ye love me, keep my commandments" (John 14:15; see also 1 John 2:3–4). Review the Ten Commandments in Exodus 20:1–17. These were not done away with in the New Testament as documented in Matthew 19:16–17, Luke 16:17, and Romans 7:7. Breaking the law willingly and knowingly is sinning (see 1 John 3:4). Christians living in the Spirit don't do that. Read Romans chapters 6 and 8. One of the commandments says, "Remember" (see Exod. 20:8) so that Christians wouldn't forget!

Day of Worship—Sabbath or Sunday?

Jesus said, "It is written, Man shall not live by bread alone, but by every word that proceedeth out of the mouth of God" (Matt. 4:4). Peter, under inspiration from God, said this: "We ought to obey God rather than men" (Acts 5:29). We shouldn't be surprised! Paul warned that false things would be coming into churches. Read for yourself 2 Timothy 4:3–5. He said, "Preach the word; be instant in season, out of season; reprove, rebuke, exhort with all long suffering and doctrine" (2 Tim. 4:2).

The church is supposed to be "the pillar and ground of the truth" (1 Tim. 3:15). " But he answered and said unto them, Why do ye also transgress the commandment of God by your tradition? This people draweth nigh unto me with their mouth, and honoureth me with their lips; but their heart is far from me. But in vain they do worship me, teaching for doctrines the commandments of men" (Matt. 15:3, 8–9).

Revelation 1:10: Under inspiration of God, John the Revelator said this: "I was in the Spirit on the Lord's day, and heard behind me a great voice, as of a trumpet." Yes, God does have a special "blessed, sanctified, and holy" day (see Gen. 2:2–3 and Exod. 20:8). Biblically, it is not Sunday—a work day (see Ezek. 46:1). It's the Lord's day, Jesus' day. So what day did Jesus worship on? The Bible tells us: "And he came to Nazareth, where he had been brought up: and, as his custom was, he went into the synagogue on the sabbath day, and stood up for to read" (Luke 4:16). "For the Son of man is Lord even of the sabbath day" (Matt. 12:8). "My holy day" (Isa. 58:13). Jesus is our example (see 1 Peter 2:21).

Biblically, we worship God because He is our Creator (see Gen. 2:1–3; Rev. 4:11; 14:6–7). No scripture in the Bible says we worship God because Jesus rose from the dead on Sunday, the first day of the week. No such scripture! Note these verses on Sabbath-keeping in the book of Acts after Jesus was resurrected and went to heaven: Acts 13:42, 44; 17:2; 18:4. Also, Matthew 24:20 was fulfilled in AD 70, many years after Jesus returned to heaven. We will be keeping the Sabbath in heaven and on the New Earth (see Isa. 66:22–23). Because no scripture exists that God changed the Sabbath to Sunday, God's day of rest still stands (see Heb.4:1–11).

Jesus Christ—The Creator of All Things

Text: "And to make all men see what is the fellowship of the mystery, which from the beginning of the world hath been hid in God, who created all things by Jesus Christ" (Eph. 3:9).

Comparison: The New International Version writes the same scripture as follows: "And to make plain to everyone the administration of this mystery, which for ages past was kept hidden in God, who created all things."

A lot of Christians don't realize that many modern translations have omitted the phrase "who created all things by Jesus Christ." In Genesis 1:1–2 it says that God created all things. Yes, He was the administrator, but His Son actually did the work! The Holy Spirit also was involved. But this truth has been omitted. Look it up for yourself.

- Good News Bible/ Today's English Version
- New English Bible

- Revised Standard Version

Comments: Serious Bible students learn that it was Jesus who created us, and He also recreates us when we are born again (see John 1:12–13; 2 Cor. 5:17; Heb. 1:2; Isa. 44:24).

The Virgin Birth

Text: "Therefore the Lord himself shall give you a sign; Behold, a virgin shall conceive, and bear a son, and shall call his name Immanuel" (Isa. 7:14).

Comparison: Other translations take away the miracle of Jesus' birth; they give Him a natural birth with a human father. For example, the Good News Bible says, "Well then, the Lord himself will give you a sign: a young woman who is pregnant will have a son and will name him Immanuel." The following versions also change the virgin birth:

- Revised Standard Version
- Today's English Version

Comments: Young women who are pregnant have sons or daughters every day—that is not a sign. The miracle is that "a virgin" shall conceive. This fact is to increase our faith.

Text: "And Joseph and his mother marvelled at those things which were spoken of him" (Luke 2:33).

Comparison: Other Bible translations give Jesus a human father, which is not the truth:

- Contemporary English Version
- Good News Bible/Today's English Version
- J.B. Phillips New Testament in Modern English

- Jerusalem Bible
- New International Version
- New World Translation of the Holy Scriptures
- Revised Standard Version

Comments: Why read a Bible that does not present the whole truth? The King James Version is faithful to the truth. Joseph was Jesus' guardian; God was His Father (Matt. 1:20; Luke 1:30–35).

Anger

Text: "But I say unto you, That whosoever is angry with his brother without a cause shall be in danger of the judgment" (Matt. 5:22).

Comparison: The New International Version says, "But I tell you that anyone who is angry with his brother will be subject to judgment." I believe that because many Bible translations omit the phrase "without a cause" there are Christians who feel unnecessarily guilty for anger that is not a sin. Please check the following translations:

- Good News Bible/ Today's English Version
- J.B. Phillips New Testament in Modern English
- The Living Bible
- New English Bible
- Revised Standard Version

Comments: By omitting words these other translations make no distinction between righteous anger and worldly anger. Paul tells us: "Be ye angry, and sin not" (Eph. 4:26).

Righteous anger (indignation) is normal for Christians who see God dishonored or misrepresented or who hear sermons that promote the false doctrine of salvation in sin, etc. If we are strong in Jesus and the Holy Spirit is controlling us, we need not have worldly anger, which is sin and subject to judgment unless we repent.

Do you prefer the encouraging truth presented in the King James Version or the unconditional false teaching of these other translations? One has hope and reality, the others condemnation regardless of circumstances. I'll take the King James Version every time because I can trust it.

Be Not Foolish and Be Not Bewitched

Text: "O foolish Galatians, who hath bewitched you, that ye should not obey the truth, before whose eyes Jesus Christ hath been evidently set forth, crucified among you?" (Gal. 3:1).

Comparison: The Revised Standard Version says, "O foolish Galatians! Who has bewitched you, before whose eyes Jesus Christ was publicly portrayed as crucified?" The phrase "that ye should not obey the truth" is omitted in most modern translations:

- Good News Bible/Today's English Version
- J.B. Phillips New Testament in Modern English
- Jerusalem Bible
- New English Bible
- New International Version
- New World Translation of the Holy Scriptures

Comments: We are foolish or bewitched (charmed, deceived) not by Jesus being crucified but in believing that we don't have to obey the truth. Titus 1:16 says, "They profess that they know God; but in works they deny him, being abominable, and disobedient, and unto every good work reprobate" (see also Jude 1:4).

We (I include myself) can all improve and ask God for more grace and wisdom to obey God's truth as we know it, such as having reverence in God's sanctuary, separating from worldliness, loving God and our fellow man, etc. Do we hate sin the way Jesus hated sin? Take a closer look at Calvary. Do we love the lost sinner enough to tell him about God's grace and salvation while probation is still open? James wrote the following under inspiration from God: "Be ye doers of the word, and not hearers only, deceiving your own selves" (James 1:22; see also Rom. 2:13).

Jesus' Second Coming

Text: "Watch therefore, for ye know neither the day nor the hour wherein the Son of man cometh" (Matt. 25:13).

Comparison: The important phrase "the Son of man cometh" is not in many modern translations. For example, the New English Bible says: "Keep awake then; for you never know neither the day or the hour." Check your Bible.

- Good News Bible/Today's English Version
- J.B. Phillips New Testament in Modern English
- Jerusalem Bible
- New International Version
- Revised Standard Version

Comments: With important words omitted, it makes a person wonder why we are to be awake and what we are to be watching for. The truth is definitely lost in this scripture. As you leave this final section, read the truths about the second coming of Jesus in 1 Thessalonians 4:13–18 and 5:23–24.

Text: And the dragon was wroth with the woman, and went to make war with the remnant of her seed, which keep the commandments of God, and have the testimony of Jesus Christ" (Rev. 12:17).

Comparison: The important word "remnant" is not found in many Bible Versions.

- Good News Bible/New English Version
- New International Version
- The New King James Version Bible
- Revised Standard Version
- Phillips Modern English

For an example, in the paraphrased Living Bible it says: "Then the furious Dragon set out to attack the rest of her children—all who were keeping God's commandments and confessing that they belong to Jesus. He stood waiting on an ocean beach."

Comment: The word "remnant" describes God's true church in these last days preparing herself to be ready and patiently waiting for Jesus' second coming. Satan doesn't like the fact that they are commandment keepers. It's love not legalism. Read John 14:15 and Revelation 22:14 in the King James Bible.

Final Thoughts

As you contemplate what you have just read, I recommend that you conduct your own historical research on the subject of how Bibles are written and where the manuscripts come from. The information is out there in books and on the Internet.

From my research, I learned that there are really only two streams of Bible translations: those based on the official version of Rome—the Sinaiticus and Vaticanus—and those written from the Received Text (also known as Textus Receptus).

The King James Version was born during the great Protestant Reformation from the original manuscripts of the Received Text. The revised versions and some modern translations have come from a mixture of about 95 percent of the Received Text and about 5 percent of the official Rome manuscripts— Sinaiticus and Vaticanus. This explains why there is a difference between the King James Version and most modern translations.

Because of the controversial nature of these truths, I recommend your own research into the subject. Other historical resources and documentation relating to how the King James Version Bible and all other modern translations came to be is available in *Which Bible?* by David Otis Fuller and a DVD titled "KJB: The Book That Changed the World" by John Rhys-Davies.

As I was driving down Interstate 95 one day, I saw a bumper sticker on the back of a car that stated, "The most violent element in society is ignorance." Right away the Holy Spirit brought three scriptures to my mind:

- "My people are destroyed for lack of knowledge" (Hosea 4:6).

- "If the foundations be destroyed, what can the righteous do?" (Ps. 11:3).

- "And ye shall know the truth, and the truth shall make you free" (John 8:32).

Bible Paraphrases

The following versions are paraphrases:

- Amplified Bible
- The Living Bible
- The Message

A paraphrase is a retelling of something in your own words, in plain everyday language. A spiritually gifted author can make Scripture come to life in a very edifying and accurate way, but there is a possibility that private interpretation and unintentional false doctrines can be introduced. To be safe, let the Holy Spirit be your Helper in understanding Scripture (John 16:13). If you like using a paraphrase, it should not be used as your primary Bible.

So why is reading the right Bible so important? Two spiritual laws or principles take place in our mind when we study God's Word and draw closer to Christ. Following are scriptures that outline these changes:

- "So shall my word be that goeth forth out of my mouth: it shall not return unto me void, but it shall accomplish that which I please, and it shall prosper in the thing whereto I sent it" (Isa. 55:11).

- "But we all, with open face beholding as in a glass the glory of the Lord, are changed into the same image from glory to glory" (2 Cor. 3:18).

- "As for me, I behold thy face in righteousness: I shall be satisfied, when I awake, with thy likeness" (Ps. 17:15).

- "Herein is our love made perfect, that we may have boldness in the day of judgment: because as he is, so are we in this world" (1 John 4:17).

Dear reader, just knowing the truth cannot help us. May we all pray for wisdom from our heavenly Counselor that will motivate us into action to make wise decisions. There is a spiritual war going on and Satan wants us to be lost. But Jesus wants us to be saved. "He restoreth my soul: he leadeth me in the paths of righteousness <u>for his name's sake</u>" (Ps. 23:3). "Nevertheless he saved them <u>for his name's sake</u>, that he might make his mighty power to be known" (Ps. 106:8). Read also Ezekiel 36:23, Isaiah 60:1–3, and *Sons and Daughters of God*, p. 242.

When the great controversy between good and evil comes to a close, God will finally be vindicated and truth will prevail. God loved us first. Now, He is asking us to love Him. "We love him, because he first loved us" (1 John 4:19). Can anyone say, **Amen**!

May grace in our life cause us to put Jesus first in our life. "For the grace of God that bringeth salvation hath appeared to all men, Teaching us that, denying ungodliness and worldly lusts, we should live soberly, righteously, and godly, <u>in this present world</u>; Looking for that blessed hope, and the glorious appearing of the great God and our Saviour Jesus Christ; Who gave himself for us [at Calvary], that he might redeem us from all iniquity, and purify unto himself a peculiar people, zealous of good works" (Titus 2:11–14, KJV).

"And every man that hath this hope in him purifieth himself, even as he is pure" (1 John 3:3). Reading about people in the Bible who were faithful to God will encourage all of us. Do you have problems and trials in life? Read the book of Job. Do you want to learn David's secret? Read Psalm 51. "Thy word have I hid in mine heart, that I might not sin against thee" (Ps. 119:11). Read about the faithful parents of John the Baptist in Luke 1:5–6. Paul made his secret clear to all of us in Romans 7:25; 8:1–39; 2 Tim. 4:7–8.

Read about the hallmark of faith in Hebrews 11 and 12:1–2, 14. We can't leave out Enoch! "And Enoch walked with God ... and he was not; for God took him" (Gen. 5:22–24). The apostle Paul wrote this: "By faith Enoch was translated that he should not see death; and was not found, because God had translated him: for before his translation he had this testimony, that he pleased God" (Heb. 11:5).

CHAPTER 10

Loyalty to God

When God gave humanity Jesus, the spotless Lamb who took the sins of the world upon Himself, He gave His Best—He gave us the truth, the whole truth, and nothing but the truth.

The title page of this book quoted the following two Scriptures: "God is light, and in him is no darkness at all" (1 John 1:5), and "Teach me thy way, O LORD; I will walk in thy truth" (Ps. 86:11). Which Bible translation most closely or correctly represents "the truth [as it] is in Jesus" (Eph. 4:21)?

It is no wonder why so many Christian churches believe so differently because we become what we read. Bible translations that mix truth with some error influence church doctrine that can be spiritually dangerous to us. We need whole, unadulterated truth to be sanctified. God's Word says, "Sanctify them through thy truth: thy word is truth" (John 17:17). Also, 1 Thessalonians 5:23–24 says, "And the very God of peace sanctify you wholly; and I pray God your whole spirit and soul and body be preserved blameless unto the coming of our Lord Jesus Christ. Faithful is he that calleth you, who also will do it." The Bible translations that have erroneous scriptures and even omit very important words of God are a misrepresentation of our Lord and Savior Jesus Christ who is the Word of God. (Read Ps. 40:7, John 1:1, and Rev. 1:1–2, 19:11–13.)

I believe that if we are loyal to God, we will believe this truth in our hearts: "The grass withereth, and the flower thereof falleth away: But the word of the Lord endureth for ever" (1 Peter 1:24–25). King David wrote, "The words of the LORD are pure words: ... Thou shalt keep them, O LORD, thou shalt preserve them from this generation for ever" (Ps. 12:6–7).

Loyalty to God demands a decision. Which Bible is the pure, preserved Word of God? We must choose a Bible we can trust to lead us to the kingdom that correctly represents the integrity of Jesus Christ, who is "the Amen, the faithful and true witness" (Rev. 3:14).

As you make your decision as to the Bible translation you will use, please consider the following three questions and scriptures:

- Is it profitable for doctrine, reproof, correction, and instruction in righteousness? Read 2 Timothy 3:16–17.

- Does it cause confusion and doubt? Or does it build our faith? Read 1 Corinthians 14:33.

- Has it been divinely preserved? God has assured us that nothing would be added or taken away to misrepresent true doctrine and saving truth? Read Psalm 12:6–7, 2 Timothy 3:15, and Revelation 22:18–20.

As Bible-believing Christians we are told in God's Word to "prove all things; hold fast that which is good" (1 Thess. 5:21). We are also told that a time is coming when sound doctrine will be pushed aside: "For the time will come when they will not endure sound doctrine; but after their own lusts shall they heap to themselves teachers, having itching ears" (2 Tim. 4:3).

As we close this study, ponder these questions:

1. Which Bible translation is the best?

2. Which Bible translation is faithful to sound doctrine? (2 Tim. 3:16–17)

3. Which Bible is the "faithful and true" witness? (Rev. 19:11–13)

Comments or Questions Welcomed

I would welcome your comments or questions. You can reach me using one of the following methods.

E-mail: rockmanrick@live.com

Phone: 443-345-1907

May we "Reason together." For Unity of Belief that God would be "Glorified" read Isaiah 1:18; John 17:9-11,17,19, 21; 1 Peter 3:8.

www.ingramcontent.com/pod-product-compliance
Lightning Source LLC
Chambersburg PA
CBHW060554100426
42742CB00013B/2552